⚜ CLASSIC
SMOCKING DESIGNS

CONTENTS

Ripples

MARSHMALLOW

All love is sweet, given or returned.

Common as light is love, and its familiar voice wearies not ever.

— PERCY BYSSHE SHELLEY —

PLEATING

Pleat twenty four full space rows (including one holding row at the bottom).

SMOCKING

Count the pleats and mark the centre valley.

Wheat stitch scallops

Wheat stitch scallops are worked between rows 21 to 22 ½ and each scallop covers twenty pleats.

Row 21 - 22 ½. Begin on the tenth and eleventh pleats to the left of the centre valley on row 21 with an over cable. Work six stepped stem stitches (thread below the needle) down to row 22 ½. Work three stem stitches and four outline stitches (thread above the needle) along row 22 ½, followed by six stepped outline stitches up to row 21. Continue to the end of the row.

Turn the fabric upside down, return to the centre and complete the row.

Complete the wheat stitch by working another row directly beneath the first. Substitute stem for outline stitch and outline for stem stitch.

Vertical ladder stitch

Vertical ladder stitch is worked over six pleats using half spaces between rows 1 to 21. The thread is kept above the needle at all times. Ensure that the needle is always horizontal.

Row 21 - 1. Turn the fabric upside down and begin at the peak of the scallops on row 21 with an over cable directly below the previous over cable. Step down to row 20 ½ and across two pleats, work an over cable, step down to row 20 and back two pleats, over cable. Continue in this manner to row 1.

Turn the fabric up the right way and work the second vertical row in the same manner as the previous row. Stitch the remaining columns of vertical ladder stitch in the same manner.

Backsmocking

The rows of scalloped backsmocking are worked on the wrong side of the fabric in a similar manner to the scalloped wheat stitch on the right side.

Row 1½ - 3. Begin on the fourth pleat to the left of the centre valley on row 3.

Work three outline and four stem stitches along row 3, six step trellis up to row 1 ½, over cable, six step trellis down to row 3. Continue to the end of the row. Turn the fabric upside down, return to the centre and complete the row.

Referring to the graph, repeat this sequence twenty times between row 2 ½ and row 23.

EMBROIDERY

Pretty bullion roses, detached chain leaves and a sprinkling of pink French knots decorate the wheat stitch scallops.

Alternating French knots and bullion rosebuds fill the diamonds formed by the vertical ladder stitch.

Work two bullion knots for the centre of each rose and surround these with five bullion knots for the petals. Add a pair of detached chain leaves on each side of the roses at the base of each scallop.

For the roses positioned just below the peaks, add one leaf on each side and a pair of leaves directly below. Scatter tiny French knots along the scallops.

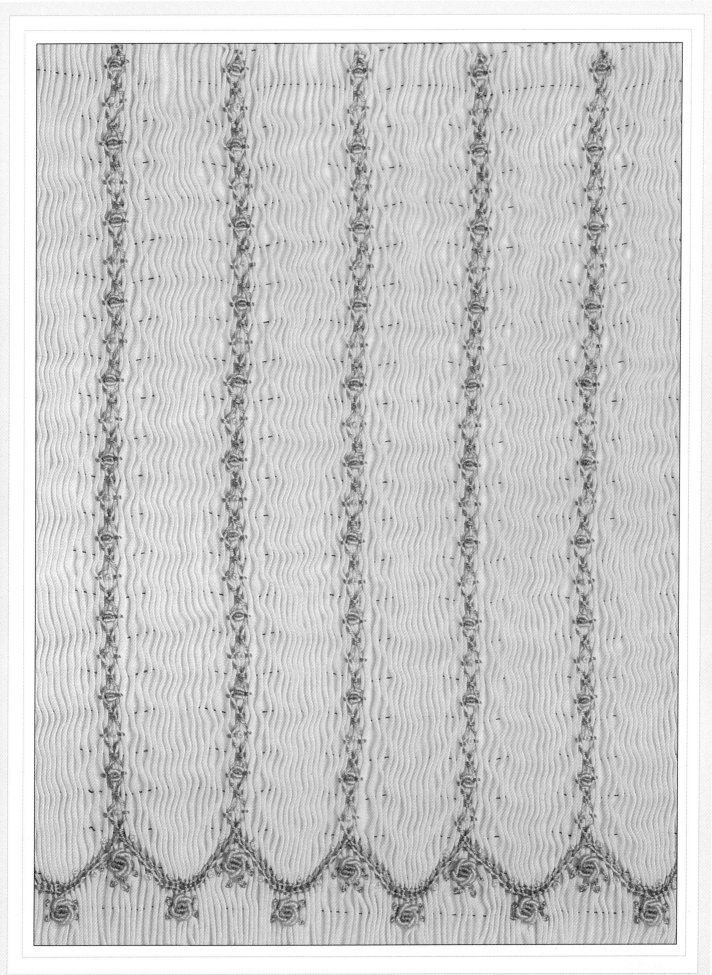

COLOUR KEY

DMC stranded cotton

A = 746 off-white

B = 776 vy lt rose

C = 818 baby pink

D = 3013 lt khaki green

Smocking = D
(3 strands)

Backsmocking = A
(2 strands)

Embroidery

Rose

Centre = B
(2 strands,
2 bullion knots,
10 wraps)

Petals = C
(2 strands,
5 bullion knots,
14 wraps)

Rosebuds

Centre = B
(2 strands, bullion
knot, 6 wraps)

Outer petals = C
(2 strands,
2 bullion knots,
10 wraps)

Spots = C
(2 strands, French
knot, 1 wrap)

Leaves = D
2 strands,
detached chain)

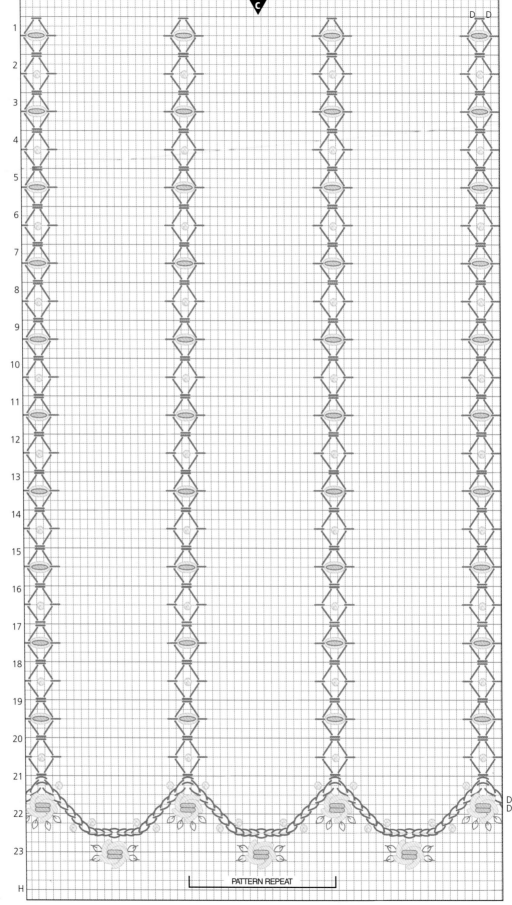

PATTERN REPEAT

BACKSMOCKING

C

PATTERN REPEAT

Wheat Stitch
~ Scallops ~

Wheat stitch is formed by working two rows of stitching close together. The upper row is outline stitch and the lower row is stem stitch. To create the scallops, a sequence combining outline and stem stitches is used for the first row. This sequence is then reversed for the second row.

BUTTERFLY *Blue*

Give your children two things ~ One is roots… the other, wings.

ANONYMOUS

PLEATING

Pleat fifteen full space rows (including two holding rows - one at the top and one at the bottom).

SMOCKING

Count the pleats and mark the centre valley.

Row 1. Begin at the centre two pleats on row 1 with an over cable and work cable to the end of the row. Turn the fabric upside down, return to the centre and complete the row.

Row 1 - 1 ¼. Begin with an over cable two pleats to the left of the centre valley and directly below the cable on row 1. Work a quarter space wave across the row. Turn the fabric upside down, return to the centre and complete the row.

Row 2 - 2 ½. Begin at the centre two pleats on row 2 with an over cable. Work wave down to row 2 ½, three cables (under, over, under), wave up to row 2. Continue to the end of the row. Turn the fabric upside down, return to the centre and complete the row.

Row 2 ½ - 3. Work a mirror image of the previous row.

Rows 3 ¾ - 4. Work a mirror image of rows 1 - 1 ¼.

Row 5 - 6. Following the graph and beginning at the centre two pleats on row 5, work six step trellis to the end of the row. Turn the fabric upside down, return to the centre and complete the row.

Rows 5 ¼ - 6 ½. Repeat the previous row twice.

Row 6 ½ - 7. Following the graph for placement, work a half space wave - seven cable combination across the row.

Rows 7 - 13. Work a mirror image of rows 1 - 7.

Accent stitches

Satin stitch bars
In the spaces between the cable and quarter space waves on rows 1, 4, 10, and 13, work satin stitch bars covering two pleats. Use two satin stitches to form each bar.

Flowerettes

Following the graph for placement, work double cable flowerettes along row six, between every alternate peak formed by the six step trellis.

To form the leaves work three stepped stem stitches (thread below the needle) around the left hand side of each flowerette. Work four stepped outline stitches (thread above the needle) below and around the right hand side of each flowerette.

Along row 8 work a mirror image of the flowerettes and stem and outline stitches following the graph for placement.

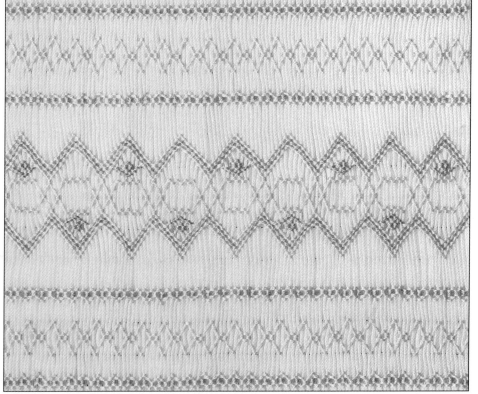

The Swallow

DMC stranded cotton

A = 524 vy lt fern green

B = 775 baby blue

C = 3325 vy lt sky blue

D = 3689 lt tea rose

Smocking = B and C

(3 strands)

Accent stitches

Satin stitch bars = C

(3 strands)

Flowerettes = D (3 strands)

Leaves = A (3 strands)

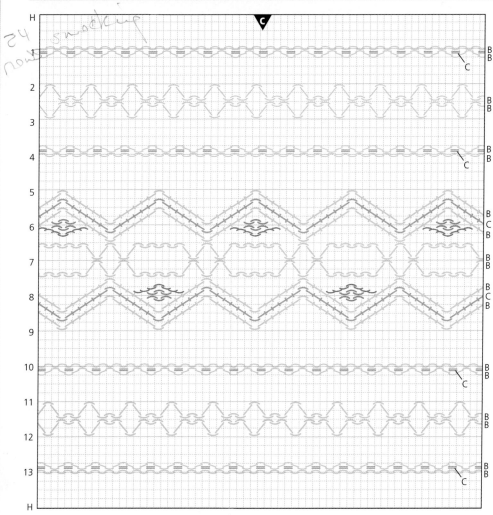

SYMPHONY OF *Roses*

O my Luve's like a red, red rose that's newly sprung in June;

O my Luve's like the melody that's sweetly play'd in tune.

— ROBERT BURNS —

PLEATING

Pleat nine full space rows (including one holding row at the top).

SMOCKING

Count the pleats and mark the centre valley.

Row 1. Begin at the centre two pleats with an over cable. Continue in cable to the end of the row. Turn the fabric upside down, return to the centre and complete the row.

Row 2 - 2 ½. Begin at the centre two pleats on row 2 with an over cable. Work two step trellis down to row 2 ½, under cable, two step trellis up to row 2. Continue to the end of the row. Turn the fabric upside down, return to the centre and complete the row.

Row 2 ½ - 3. Work a mirror image of the previous row.

Rows 3 - 5. Repeat rows 2 - 3 twice.

Row 5 - 5 ½. Using the medium pink thread, repeat the previous row a half space below.

Row 5 ½ - 6. Using the darkest pink thread, repeat the previous row.

Row 6 - 7. Begin at the centre two pleats on row 7 with an under cable. Work five step trellis up to row 6, over cable, five step trellis down to row 7. Continue to the end of the row. Turn the fabric upside down, return to the centre and complete the row.

Row 6 ½ - 7 ½. Using the medium pink thread, repeat row 6 - 7.

EMBROIDERY

Bullion rosebuds, with detached chain leaves, are worked over eight pleats along row 3 ½, across the centre of every third diamond.

Each bud is worked over four pleats and each detached chain leaf over two pleats.

Work the centre petal of the bud first, followed by the outer petals, then the detached chain leaves, one at each end of the bud.

COLOUR KEY

DMC stranded cotton

A = 524 vy lt fern green

B = 3687 tea rose

C = 3688 med tea rose

D = 3689 lt tea rose

Smocking = B, C and D (3 strands)

Embroidery

Rosebuds

Centre = B (2 strands, bullion knot, 8 wraps)

Outer petals = D (2 strands, 2 bullion knots, 14 wraps)

Leaves = A (2 strands, detached chain)

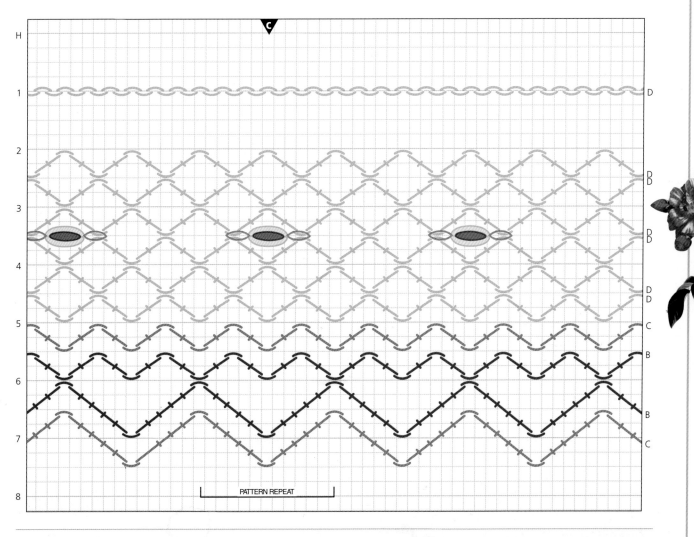

PATTERN REPEAT

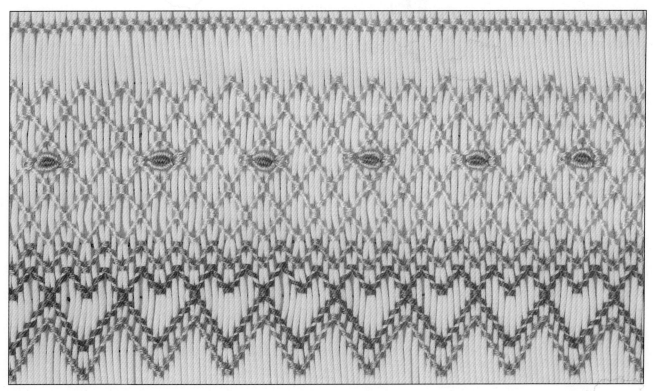

DREAMSCAPE

I love the simple things of life,

A bright log fire, soft candlelight...

A poster bed to dream at night.

LUCILLE McBROOM CRUMLEY

PLEATING

Pleat eighteen full space rows (including two holding rows - one at the top and one at the bottom).

SMOCKING

Count the pleats and mark the centre valley.

Row ¹/₂ - 1. Begin at the centre two pleats on row 1 with an under cable. Wave up to row ¹/₂, over cable, wave down to row 1. Continue working half space wave to the end of the row. Turn the fabric upside down, return to the centre and complete the row.

Rows 1 - 2. Repeat row ¹/₂ - 1 twice, changing the colour of the thread for each row.

Rows 9 - 10 ¹/₂. Work a mirror image of rows ¹/₂ - 2.

Row 10 ¹/₂ - 11. Following the graph work a mirror image of row 10 - 10 ¹/₂.

Row 11 - 11 ¹/₂. Work a mirror image of the previous row.

Rows 11 ¹/₂ - 14 ¹/₂. Repeat rows 10 ¹/₂ - 11 ¹/₂ three times, forming diamonds.

Rows 14 ¹/₂ - 16. Repeat rows ¹/₂ - 2.

Backsmocking

Following the graph for placement, backsmock between rows 2 - 9 in four step trellis.

Accent stitches

Satin stitch bars, subtly placed among the baby wave diamonds, create a larger diamond design around the rosebuds.

The satin stitch bars are formed by working two satin stitches over two pleats. Carefully follow the graph for placement.

EMBROIDERY

Pink bullion rosebuds with detached chain leaves are worked in the centre of the diamonds on row 12 ¹/₂.

The buds are worked over two pleats and a detached chain leaf, over two pleats, is worked on each side of the rosebuds. Work the buds first, followed by the leaves.

Satin stitch bars, subtly placed among the baby wave diamonds, create a larger diamond design around the rosebuds.

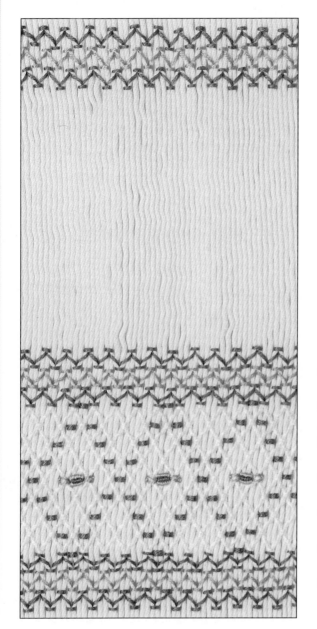

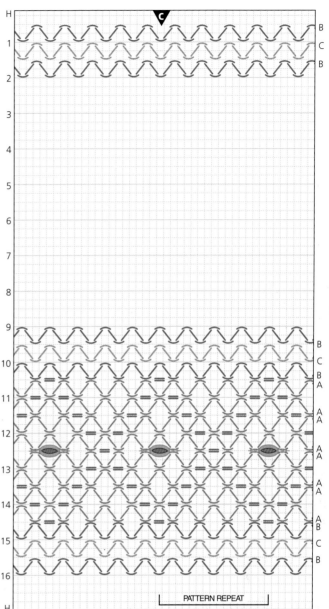

Colour Key

DMC stranded cotton

A = blanc

B = 501 dk blue-green

C = 503 med blue-green

D = 3726 dk antique mauve

E = 3727 lt antique mauve

Smocking = A, B and C (3 strands)

Backsmocking = A (2 strands)

Accent stitches

Satin stitch bars = B (2 strands)

Embroidery

Rosebuds

Centre = D (2 strands, bullion knot, 8 wraps)

Outer petals = E (2 strands, 2 bullion knots, 12 wraps)

Leaves = C (2 strands, detached chain)

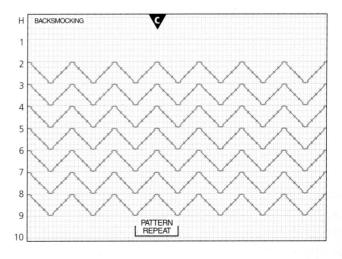

Whispers

SWEET

Wise sayings often fall on barren ground,
but a kind word is never thrown away.

SIR ARTHUR HELPS

PLEATING

Pleat twenty full space rows (including two holding rows - one at the top and one at the bottom).

SMOCKING

Count the pleats and mark the centre valley.

Row 1. Begin at the centre two pleats on row 1 with an over cable. Continue in cable to the end of the row. Turn the fabric upside down, return to the centre and complete the row.

Row 2. Repeat the previous row.

Row 1 1/2 - 2. Begin at the centre two pleats on row 1 1/2 with an over cable. Wave down to row 2, under cable, wave up to row 1 1/2. Continue to the end of the row. Turn the fabric upside down, return to the centre and complete the row.

Row 3. Work a row of cable in exactly the same manner as row 1.

To work the alternating cables, begin with an over cable directly below the cable on row 3 and two pleats to the left of the centre valley. Work two more cables (under, over).

Take the needle to the back of the fabric, re-emerging directly above the next over cable on row 3. Work three cables (under, over, under).

Continue with this sequence to the end of the row. Turn the fabric upside down, return to the centre and complete the row.

Row 4 - 4 1/2. Beginning at the centre two pleats with an under cable on row 4 1/2, work two step trellis across the row. Turn the fabric upside down, return to the centre and complete the row.

Row 4 1/2 - 5. Work a mirror image of the previous row.

Rows 3 1/2 - 4 and 5 - 5 1/2. Referring carefully to the graph and beginning four pleats to the left of the centre valley, work a set of two step trellis to form a diamond below row 5. Carry the thread vertically on the back of the fabric and complete a two step trellis diamond above row 4. Continue in this manner to the end of the row. Turn the fabric upside down, return to the centre and complete the row.

Rows 6 - 6 1/2. Work a mirror image of rows 1 1/2 - 2.

Row 7 - 7 1/2. The trailing vine is formed by working four straight outline stitches and four stepped outline stitches over a half space row. Refer carefully to the graph for stitch placement. Outline stitch is always worked with the thread above the needle.

Row 7 1/2 - 8. Work a mirror image of the previous row, substituting stem stitch for the outline stitch. Stem stitch is always worked with the thread below the needle.

Rows 8 1/2 - 9. Work a mirror image of rows 6 - 6 1/2.

Rows 10 - 11. Repeat rows 4 - 5.

Row 9 1/2 - 10. Referring carefully to the graph, work a set of two step trellis to form a diamond above row 9 1/2. Backsmock in cable on the wrong side of the fabric and re-emerge above the next over cable of the row below. Continue in this manner to the end of the row.

Row 11 - 11 1/2. Work a mirror image of row 9 1/2 - 10.

Rows 12 - 12 1/2. Work a mirror image of rows 8 1/2 - 9.

Rows 13 - 14. Repeat rows 7 - 8.

Rows 14 1/2 - 15. Work a mirror image of rows 12 - 12 1/2.

Rows 15 1/2 - 17 1/2. Repeat rows 3 1/2 - 5 1/2.

Row 18. Repeat row 3.

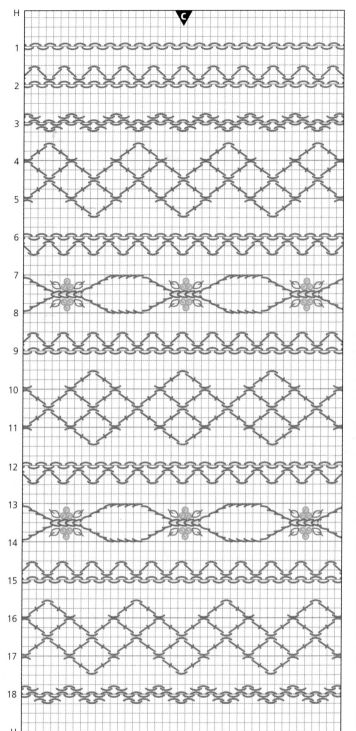

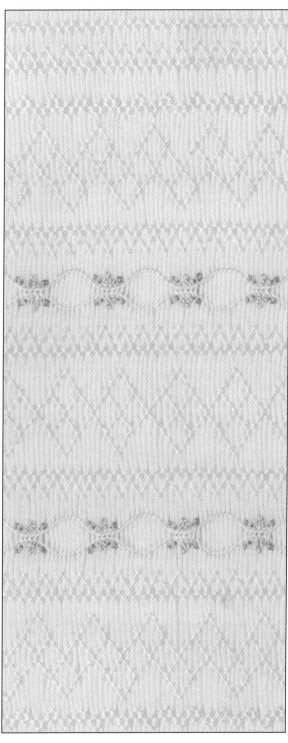

EMBROIDERY

Tiny leaves and French knot buds are worked along the outer edges of the trailing vines.

Embroider the groups of three French knot buds first, referring to the graph for placement. Work the detached chain leaves over two pleats, stitching a leaf on each side of each group of buds.

COLOUR KEY

DMC stranded cotton

A = 503 med

blue-green

B = 746 off-white

C = 3713 vy lt salmon

Smocking = B (3 strands)

Embroidery

Buds = C (3 strands,

French knot, 1 wrap)

Leaves = A (2 strands,

detached chain)

Prudence

DEARE

Live and work but do not forget to play,

to have fun in life and really enjoy it.

EILEEN CADDY

PLEATING

Pleat twelve full space rows (including two holding rows - one at the top and one at the bottom).

SMOCKING

Count the pleats and mark the centre valley.

Base rows

Row 1 - 1 ½. Begin on the first and second pleats to the left of the centre valley with an over cable. Work two more cables (under, over) wave down to row 1 ½, three cables along row 1 ½ (under, over, under) wave up to row 1. Continue to the end of the row.

Turn the fabric upside down, return to the centre and complete the row.

Row 1 ½ - 2. Work a mirror image of the previous row.

Rows 2 - 3. Repeat rows 1 - 2, using the cream thread.

Rows 3 - 4. Repeat rows 2 - 3, using the blue thread.

Rows 7 - 10. Work a mirror image of the base rows between rows 1 and 4.

Pink crossover rows

Row 1 - 1 ½. Begin on the third and fourth pleats to the right of the centre valley with an over cable. Work two more cables (under, over) wave

down to row 1 ½, three cables along row 1 ½ (under, over, under) wave up to row 1. Continue to the end of the row. Turn the fabric upside down, return to the centre and complete the row.

Row 1 ½ - 2. Work a mirror image of the previous row.

Rows 2 - 4. Repeat rows 1 - 2 twice.

Rows 2 - 10. Repeat rows 1 - 2 eight times.

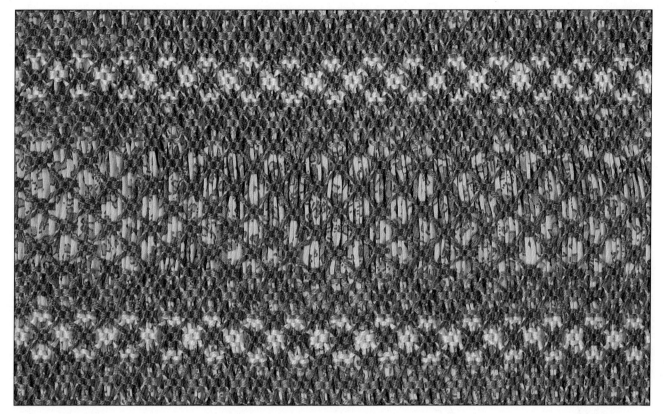

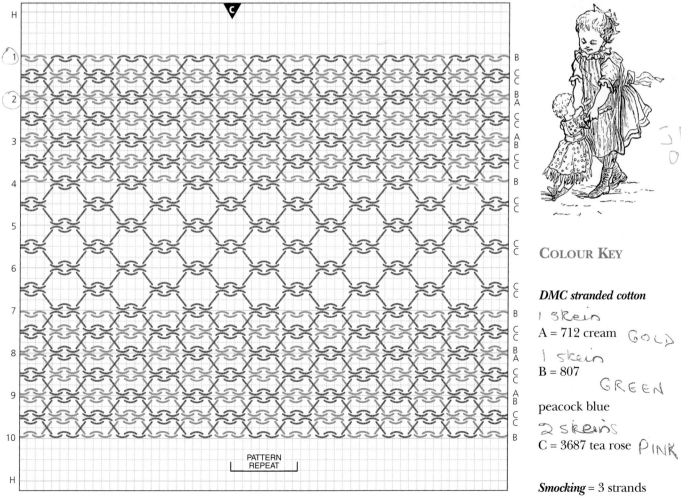

H

C

1

2

3

4

5

6

7

8

9

10

H

B
C C
B A
C C
B A
C C
B
C C
C C
C C
B
C C
B A
C C
A B
C C
B

PATTERN
REPEAT

COLOUR KEY

DMC stranded cotton

1 skein
A = 712 cream GOLD

1 skein
B = 807

GREEN

peacock blue

2 skeins
C = 3687 tea rose PINK

Smocking = 3 strands

PRECIOUS Angel

Precious angel, under the sun,

 How was I to know you'd be the one.

— BOB DYLAN —

PLEATING

Pleat twenty one full space rows (including two holding rows - one at the top and one at the bottom).

SMOCKING

Count the pleats and mark the centre valley.

Row 1. Using the light blue thread, begin at the centre two pleats on row 1 with an under cable. Work cable to the end of the row. Turn the fabric upside down, return to the centre and complete the row.

Using the darker blue thread, begin two pleats to the left of the centre valley with an under cable, directly above the light blue cable on row 1. Work a further two cables (over, under).

Take the needle to the back of the fabric, re-emerging directly below the next light blue under cable on row 1.

Work three cables (over, under, over). Take the needle to the back of the fabric, re-emerging directly above the next light blue over cable on row 1.

Continue with this sequence to the end of the row. Turn the fabric upside down, return to the centre and complete the row.

Row 2 - 2 1/2. Begin at the centre two pleats on row 2 1/2 with an under cable. Wave up to row 2, over cable, wave down to row 2 1/2. Continue to the end of the row. Turn the fabric upside down, return to the centre and complete the row.

Row 2 1/2 - 3. Work a mirror image of the previous row.

Rows 1 1/2 - 2 and 3 - 3 1/2. Using the darker blue thread, begin on the third pleat to the left of the centre valley on row 2 with an under cable, wave up to row 1 1/2, over cable, wave down to

row 2, under cable. Carry the thread vertically on the back of the fabric re-emerging on row 3, directly below the under cable of the previous row. Work an over cable, wave down to row 3 1/2, under cable, wave up to row 3, over cable. Carry the thread vertically on the back of the fabric, re-emerging on row 2, directly above the next over cable. Continue to the end of the row. Turn the fabric upside down, return to the centre and complete the row.

Row 4. Using the light blue thread and following the graph for placement, work cable across the row.

Row 4 - 4 1/2. Using the darker blue thread and following the graph for placement, work half space wave, three cable combination across the row.

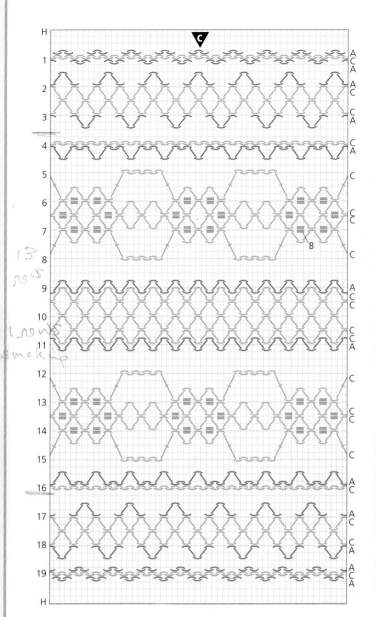

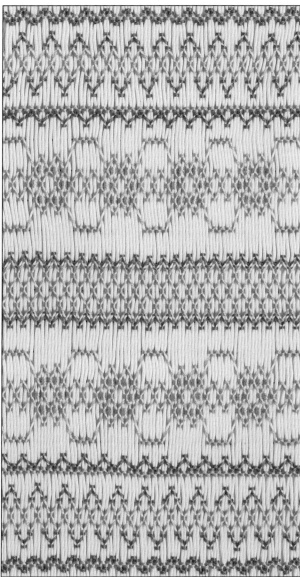

Row 5 - 6. Using the lighter blue thread, begin at the centre two pleats on row 6 with an under cable. Wave up to row 5 $\frac{1}{2}$, over cable, wave down to row 6, under cable, two step trellis up to row 5. Work seven cables, beginning with an over cable, two step trellis down to row 6, under cable, wave up to row 5 $\frac{1}{2}$, over cable, wave down to row 6. Continue in this manner to the end of the row. Turn the fabric upside down, return to the centre and complete the row.

Row 6 - 6 $\frac{1}{2}$. Following the graph for placement, work half space wave across the row.

Rows 6 $\frac{1}{2}$ - 8. Work a mirror image of rows 5 - 6 $\frac{1}{2}$.

Row 9 - 9 $\frac{1}{2}$. Following the graph for placement, work half space wave across the row.

Row 9 $\frac{1}{2}$ - 10. Work a mirror image of row 9 - 9 $\frac{1}{2}$.

Row 8 $\frac{3}{4}$ - 9 $\frac{1}{4}$. Using the darker blue thread, work a row of half space wave directly above row 9 - 9 $\frac{1}{2}$.

Rows 10 - 19. Work a mirror image of rows 1 - 10.

Accent stitches

Following the graph for placement, work pink satin stitch bars over two pleats in the centre of selected diamonds on rows 6, 6 $\frac{1}{2}$ and 7 and also on rows 13, 13 $\frac{1}{2}$ and 14.

Colour Key

DMC stranded cotton

A = 322 dk sky blue

B = 776 vy lt rose

C = 3755 lt sky blue

Smocking = A and C (3 strands)

Accent stitches

Satin stitch bars = B (3 strands)

FOREVER
Young

Happy songs by lovers sung, Long ago when Time was young

JOSEPHINE POWELL BEATY

PLEATING

Pleat eighteen full space rows (including two holding rows - one at the top and one at the bottom).

SMOCKING

Count the pleats and mark the centre valley.

Row 1. Begin at the centre two pleats on row 1 with an under cable. Continue working cable to the end of the row. Turn the fabric upside down, return to the centre and complete the row.

Row 2. Repeat the previous row.

Row 3 - 3 ½. Begin at the centre two pleats on row 3 with an over cable. Work wave down to row 3 ½, under cable, wave up to row 3. Continue working half space wave to the end of the row. Turn the fabric upside down, return to the centre and complete the row.

Row 3 ½ - 4. Work a mirror image of the previous row.

Rows 2 ½ - 3 and 4 - 4 ½. Beginning five pleats to the left of the centre valley on row 3, work an under cable, half space wave, over cable. Continue until two diamonds are formed between rows 2 ½ and 3.

Carrying the thread vertically on the back of the fabric, bring it to the front four pleats to the right of the centre valley on row 4. Work an over cable. This over cable uses the same two pleats as the previous under cable. Continue the wave pattern until three diamonds are formed.

Carrying the thread on the back of the fabric, bring it to the front on row 3, ready to work an under cable over the same two pleats as the previous over cable.

Referring to the graph, continue in the same manner to the end of the row. Turn the fabric upside down, return near the centre and complete the row.

Rows 5 and 6. Work a mirror image of rows 1 and 2.

Rows 6 ½ - 7. Using the darker green thread, begin at the centre two pleats on row 6 ½ with an under cable. Work two step trellis across the row.

Turn the fabric upside down, return to the centre and complete the row.

Using the medium green thread, repeat the previous row a quarter space below.

Using the light green thread, repeat the previous row a quarter space below, in the same manner.

Row 8 - 9. Begin at the second pleat to the left of the centre valley on row 9. With the thread above the needle, work five outline stitches along row 9, six outline stitches up to row 8, five outline stitches along row 8, then six outline stitches down to row 9. Continue in this manner to the end of the row. Turn the fabric upside down, return to the centre and complete the row.

Rows 9 ½ - 16. Work a mirror image of rows 1 - 7 ½.

Accent stitches

Flowerettes

Following the graph for placement, work the double cable flowerettes along row 8.

Work the groups of three single flowerettes between rows 8 ½ and 9. Complete one set and end off the thread before beginning the next set.

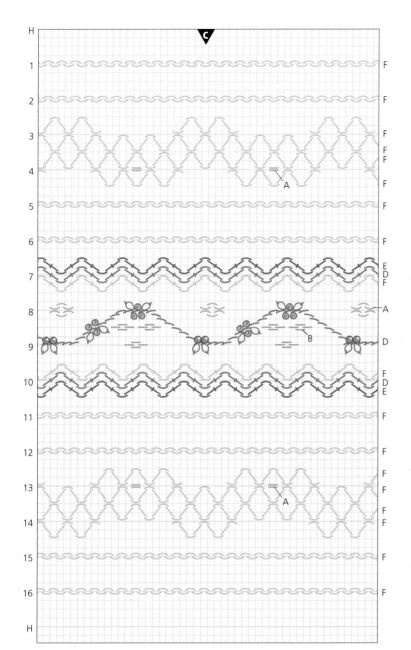

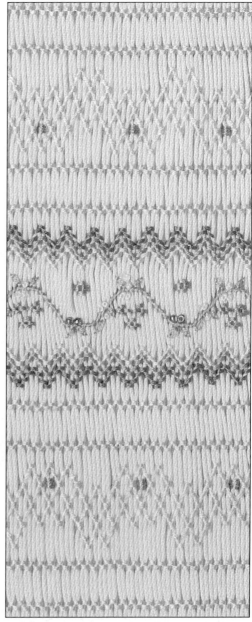

Satin stitch bars

Following the graph for placement, work the satin stitch bars over two pleats along rows 4 and 13, in the centre diamond of the sets of three diamonds.

EMBROIDERY

Tiny leaves and French knot buds are embroidered along the trailing vine. Pairs of seed beads embellish the vine.

Embroider the groups of three French knot buds first, referring to the graph for placement. Work the pairs of detached chain leaves and attach the seed beads.

COLOUR KEY

DMC stranded cotton

A = 224 vy lt shell pink

B = 3042 lt antique violet

C = 3078 vy lt golden yellow

Anchor stranded cotton

D = 875 lt blue-green

E = 876 blue-green

F = 1042 vy lt blue-green

Mill Hill glass seed beads

G = 02024 heather mauve

Smocking = D, E and F (3 strands)

Accent stitches = A and B (3 strands)

Embroidery

Buds = C (3 strands, French knot, 1 wrap)

Leaves = D (2 strands, detached chain)

UNREQUITED Love

Sweet face of love, please do not pass me by;

but trade me kiss for kiss, and sigh for sigh.

~ BERNARD W. MANN ~

PLEATING

Pleat seven full space rows (including two holding rows - one at the top and one at the bottom).

SMOCKING

Count the pleats and mark the centre valley.

Row 1. Begin at the centre two pleats on row 1 with an under cable. Continue in cable to the end of the row. Turn the fabric upside down, return to the centre and complete the row.

Above row 1. Work a mirror image of row 1 directly above the previous cable row.

Row 1 1/2. Work a row of outline stitch (thread above the needle).

Work a row of stem stitch (thread below the needle) directly below the row of outline stitch.

Row 2. Repeat row 1.

Row 2 - 2 1/2. Begin at the centre two pleats on row 2 1/2 with an under cable. Work half space wave up to row 2, over cable, half space wave down to row 2 1/2. Continue to the end of the row.

Turn the fabric upside down, return to the centre and complete the row.

Row 2 1/2 - 3. Work a mirror image of the previous row.

Rows 3 - 4. Repeat the previous two rows.

Rows 4 - 5 1/2. Refer carefully to the graph for the placement of the sets of half space waves. Work three half space waves in the first row, two in the second row and one in the third row. Complete one set and end off the thread before beginning the next set.

COLOUR KEY

DMC stranded cotton

A = 931 med antique blue

Smocking = 3 strands

Outstrip the winds my courier dove!
On pinions fleet and free.
And bear this letter to my love
Who's far away from me.

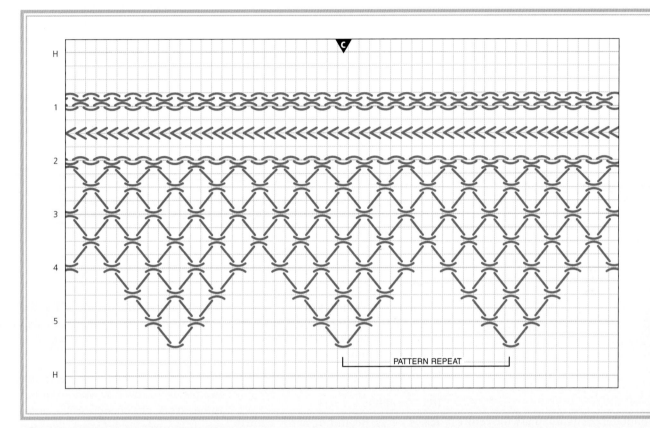

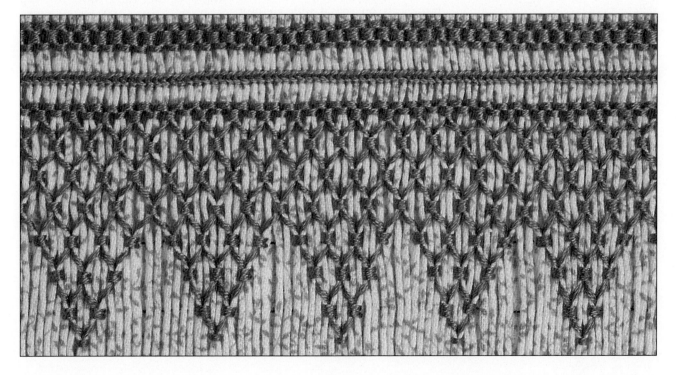

FAIRY Floss

Come up here, O dusty feet! Here is fairy bread to eat...

And when you have eaten well, Fairy stories hear and tell.

ROBERT LOUIS STEVENSON

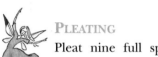

PLEATING

Pleat nine full space rows (including two holding rows - one at the top and one at the bottom).

SMOCKING

Count the pleats and mark the centre valley.

Row 1. Work a row of outline stitch (thread above the needle).

Work a row of stem stitch (thread below the needle) directly below the previous outline stitch.

Row 1 1/2 - 2. Begin at the centre two pleats on row 1 1/2 with an over cable. Work wave down to row 2, under cable, wave up to row 1 1/2. Continue to the end of the row. Turn the fabric upside down, return to the centre and complete the row.

Row 2 - 2 1/2. Repeat the previous row.

Row 2 1/2 - 3 1/4. Following the graph and beginning at the centre with an under cable on row 3, work a combination of half space wave, three step trellis to the end of the row.

Row 3 1/4 - 4. Beginning on row 4 and leaving eleven pleats free to the right

of the centre valley, work an under cable. Work five step trellis up to row 3 1/4, over cable, five step trellis down to row 4. Continue to the end of the row. Turn the fabric upside down, leaving eleven pleats from the centre free, complete the row.

Row 4 - 4 1/2. Beginning at the centre two pleats on row 4 with an over cable, work two step trellis to the end of the row. Turn the fabric upside down, return to the centre and complete the row.

Row 4 1/2 - 5. Work a mirror image of the previous row.

Row 5 - 5 1/2. Repeat row 4 - 4 1/2.

Centre of rows 5 1/2 - 6. Begin ten pleats to the left of the centre valley on row 5 1/2 with an over cable. Work two step trellis until three diamonds are formed.

Row 6 - 6 1/2. Turn the fabric upside down. Beginning seven pleats from the centre valley, work two step trellis until two diamonds are formed.

Row 6 1/2 - 7. Beginning four pleats to the left of the centre valley, work two step trellis to complete a single diamond.

Sides of row 5 1/2 - 6. Following the graph for placement, work two step trellis to create a diamond from every alternate peak.

Row 5 1/2 - 7 1/2. Begin at the centre two pleats on row 7 1/2 with an under cable. Work eleven step trellis up to row 5 1/2, over cable. Work five step trellis down to row 6 1/2, under cable. Continue working five step trellis to the end of the row. Turn the fabric upside down, return to the centre and complete the row.

EMBROIDERY

A dusky pink bullion rose, rosebuds, detached chain leaves and French knots are worked on row 3 1/2, in the space created by the smocking design.

The rose is worked over six pleats, the buds over four pleats and the detached chain leaves over two pleats.

Work the centre of the rose first and surround this with two rounds of petals. Stitch the buds next, then the leaves. Finally stitch the pink French knots.

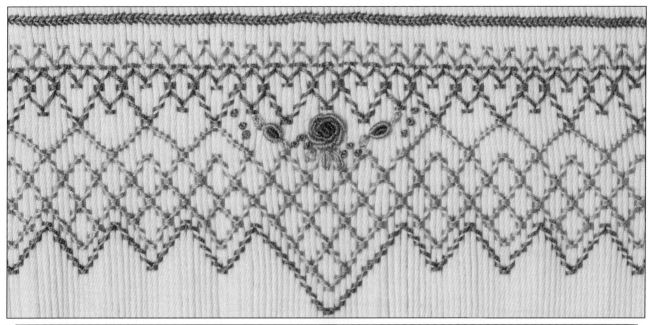

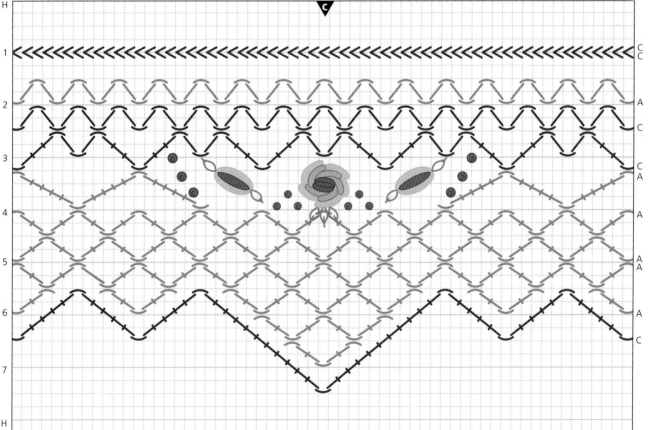

COLOUR KEY

DMC stranded cotton

A = 3354 lt dusky rose

B = 3687 tea rose

C = 3688 med tea rose

D = 3817 lt seagreen

Smocking = A and C (3 strands)

Embroidery

Rose

Centre = B (2 strands, 3 bullion knots, 8 wraps)

Inner petals = C (2 strands, 5 bullion knots, 12 wraps)

Outer petals = A (2 strands, 5 bullion knots, 12 wraps)

Rosebuds

Centre = B (2 strands, bullion knot, 6 wraps)

Petals = A (2 strands, 2 bullion knots, 12 wraps)

Leaves = D (2 strands, detached chain)

Dots = C (2 strands, French knot, 1 wrap)

~ SPECIAL THANKS TO ~

Sue Batterham, Louisa Cooper, Carol Cullen, Margaret Herzfeld

and Joyleen Miller for the original designs, and to Robyn Beaver,

Marian Carpenter, Andrew Dunbar, Lizzie Kulinski,

Lahn Stafford Design, Heidi Reid and Fiona Wynne

for their tireless efforts in bringing this book to fruition.